Live
Fearless

5 Ways to Overcome Fear and Become
Unstoppable

Charletta   Adams

Copyright

Scripture quotations taken from the Amplified®
Bible, Copyright © 1954, 1958, 1962, 1964, 1965,
1987 by The Lockman Foundation Used by
permission. (www.Lockman.org)

Scripture taken from the New King James Version®.
Copyright © 1982 by Thomas Nelson, Inc. Used by
permission. All rights reserved.
ISBN: 0996046402
ISBN-13: 978-0996046404

Sondra,
Thank you so much for being here. You're such a blessing! It was a pleasure to meet you! God bless you!
Charlotte

DEDICATION

This book is dedicated to my children. The three reasons I have to continue to overcome fear daily.

Also to my parents who taught me to be fearless.

Sandra,

Thank you so much for being kind. You're such a blessing. It was a pleasure to meet you! God bless you!

Chantitte

Contents

ACKNOWLEDGMENTS

Thank you to the following people for their contributions to my inspiration, knowledge, and other help in creating this book:

First and foremost, I'd like to thank God because without Him, I wouldn't have had the strength and courage to write this book.

Thank you to my amazing children. Your patience and encouragement has meant so much to me.

An extra special thanks to Alyssa, Andrew, Arinetta, Clair, Felicia, Fran and Nate. You opened your heart and soul for me.

Additionally, I'd like to thank my mentor and friend, Michelle Moore. Thank you for everything. Including pushing me when I was procrastinating! My editor, Alice Sullivan – thank you for such patience and amazing work! Patrick Collins- my awesome photographer. Montagne, thank you for letting me bounce ideas off you. The people in the *Writing with Purpose* class especially Carla, my wonderful friends, Nioshi, Starr, Jhiquita, Margo, Sandy, Reba, Rosetta, James, Fran, Petrina, and Becky. And to everyone who believed in my blogs and encouraged me.

INTRODUCTION

As a speaker and business coach, I hear individuals recite reasons why their fears hold them back. It's staggering how many men and women will never use their God-given talents to achieve the very things they were created for because of their fears. Inside this book lies needed information to help you crush fear like a cockroach and learn what it takes to regain the power you have given away to fear.

Have you ever been so paralyzed by fear that you practically black out? Your palms are suddenly sweaty and your heart is racing uncontrollably from the discomfort. Whether you have small fears, large fears, or somewhere in between, Live Fearless covers proven techniques and tips you can use each step of the way to conquer the very things that are holding you back.

Each chapter gives short, no-nonsense, and to-the-point information and techniques. This is balanced by understanding how fear operates within us and how we can react unreasonably to the fears we have. Each chapter ends with questions to guide you through overcoming fears.

I first met Charletta in a writing class I was teaching at our church. At the time, Charletta dreamed of being an author. A few times she even shared about how she planned to become a speaker and continue her life coaching business. Helping her clients is clearly something she is passionate about. I loved watching her and seeing how she'd smile whenever she would let herself dare to dream of becoming an author.

Inevitably, like most I speak with who have big aspirations and goals, the conversation would take a turn to her concerns. Those concerns were really fears she had about not knowing how to write and publish a book, and having the bravery to speak from a stage. I reminded her of how Theodore Roosevelt once famously said something that applied to her situation: "Believe you can and you're halfway there." However, that is something very difficult to achieve while gripped with fear. I am happy to report that I have watched Charletta grow and walk out the very path she coaches and speaks about to so many. She has done what so many never achieve by writing and publishing her first book!

If you plan on achieving the greatness down inside you, fear must be dealt with. So grab your commitment, gather up your determination, and use this step-by-step book as a compass to guide yourself along the path to reaching heights you've never seen! There really is no better time to get started than the present.

~ Michelle Moore, Award-winning Author and Charletta's Mentor

Prosperity is not without many fears and distastes; adversity not without many comforts and hopes.

~ Francis Bacon

CHAPTER 1

WHAT CAUSES FEAR?

When someone mentions the word fear, what come to mind?

The word fear brings about many things. There's a "healthy" fear of bugs, snakes, heights, scary movies, and things of that nature. What I mean by healthy is that it's very common; healthy fear is a natural response to something that can cause us harm. If I see a spider, I'm running for the hills. At the same time, this fear does not keep me from moving forward in my life. If I see a spider, I run, scream, and get someone to kill it. Then life is normal again.

Another normal, healthy fear is of heights. An estimated 31.3 million people in the U.S. are afraid of heights. That's a lot of people! These people generally avoid ladders, skydiving, and the high dive at pools. Other than those minor limitations, they live perfectly normal lives.

Trust me; you are not alone when it comes to fears. However, these kinds of fears should not keep you from living a healthy, normal life.

On the other hand, there is another kind of fear that has total control over our lives. No matter what we do, this paralyzing, unhealthy fear grips us and renders us incapable of doing whatever it is we're trying to accomplish.

Have you ever felt that way? Have you been so terrified of something that you've done everything in your power to avoid doing it? You procrastinate and you make excuses for why you can't do it. You worry, toss, and turn. You try not to dwell on it, but there it is, consuming your thoughts and your life. It could be a fear about your finances, health, relationships, or your career. So what is causing this fear?

The dictionary describes fear as a distressing emotion aroused by impending danger, evil, or pain. Whether the threat is real or imagined, it produces the feeling of being afraid. That's right—fear can cause stress even if the fear is imagined! Either way, it can lead to some serious health problems. You really don't want that to be your fate, do you?

Sometimes I look at the children in my neighborhood and I'm completely amazed at how fearless they are. They will try anything! I remember the calls I received from teachers when my own kids had done something daring and ended up in the emergency room.

Much like a child, you need to embrace a fearless attitude. Your goal probably won't land you in the E.R. But it will require that you spread your wings a little. The key is to be fearless when it comes to our goals and dreams.

MYTH – Most fears are rational.

FACT – We allow our minds to grow the fear to an irrational state. According to statisticbrain.com, 90 percent of people are afraid of things that are considered to be insignificant issues.

There is no single cause of fear. In fact, there could be several factors. Most likely these factors are playing a major role in what's causing your fear. You may be in a stressful situation or you may have suffered a traumatic event. For example, you may have suffered from fears or anxieties as a child. Growing up, my mom was terrified of water. When she was little, she had an incident where she almost drowned. After that, she would not even take showers because she felt like she was drowning. But she faced her fear through us. She didn't want me or my siblings to have that fear so she made sure we all got swimming lessons. We loved being in the water! Our courage in the water helped her confront her fears. When she got older, she was able to take showers; she just learned not to let the water get in her face.

What about fears that sound irrational? I have a co-worker who recently admitted she has a fear of success. It sounds crazy, doesn't it? But it's not; a lot of people are afraid of succeeding. You would think someone with this fear would look forward to getting everything they've wanted. Yet this fear can be immobilizing. When she got to a certain level of success in her business, she had a panic attack! She was so terrified of getting what she wanted in her career, just thinking about reaching this major level of success made her heart race, she couldn't breathe, and she couldn't even think straight. This was all because of thoughts she was having. Nothing happened to her in real life that gave her a reason to react like this; it was all in her mind. This is what fear is capable of doing.

MYTH – People are not held captive by their fears of rejection, failure, and not belonging.

FACT – We allow our minds to grow to an irrational state.

A dear friend of mine experienced a life-changing fear. She was casually dating someone when she found out she was pregnant. She was not ready to get married, and had some extremely important decisions to make. She decided to keep the baby and has never regretted that decision. Has it been tough? Very. Has she been afraid? Of course. But she didn't let it stop her from moving forward, taking charge of the situation, and doing what she needed to do.

Not everyone can handle the responsibility of being a single mother. Over the years, she's faced many challenges and fears, and I'm sure there will be many more. But she's not afraid to face what's ahead. It's very easy to blame someone else when we're facing fears and issues we don't necessarily want to deal with. The most stressful time of my life was when I was going through my divorce. At first, I blamed my ex-husband for the marriage falling apart.

I didn't want to face the things that were my fault, and I had many fears. For one, I was afraid of starting over at thirty-nine. I had been with my ex-husband since I was fifteen years old—literally more than half of my life! I had gone from living with my parents, to living with my husband—and here I was starting over. Next, I feared being a single mom. The stress of finding a new place to live was terrifying. My kids were also in a good school system and I wanted to keep them there. That was another challenge. We lived in a small town with few housing options. I was also very afraid of the affects it would have on my children, and I wanted to keep their lives as normal as possible.

I was afraid of handling the finances on my own. I had never paid all the bills or was the only source of income. It was a very stressful situation! But I got through it. I'm not going to tell you it was all roses either, because it wasn't. There were some really bad days. But I'm a much better person now than I was then. I still deal with fears, but I'm better prepared now, and being better prepared has made a big difference.

Fear is a self-limiting belief. What does that mean? It means that there are things that you believe about yourself that place limitations on your abilities. They may be real or imagined. An example would be this statement: "I'm a single mom with five kids, so no one will marry me." The fact that you're a single mom is true. The thought that no one will marry you is a self-limiting belief. There are lots of men who marry single mothers.

The limitations that exist in your mind cause you to fear. Using the example above, if you truly believed that you're never going to marry again because you're a single mom, your thoughts are telling you this daily and reinforcing this lie. Soon, you start to believe it, and you give up trying to find someone because you've completely convinced yourself that you can't find anyone. You're afraid to even try. So how can you overcome fear?

When fear tries to take over, go back to a time of victory; a time when you conquered fear and persevered. If you did it then, you can do it now! Fear can limit our abilities to become who we are destined to be. When we struggle with fear, it unconsciously sabotages our habits, beliefs, and attitudes.

While fear can be overwhelming, it doesn't mean you can't take control of it and conquer it. Whatever it is, if it's holding you back, you need to overcome it so you can move forward. You should not allow your thoughts and fears to justify why you're not growing and evolving. When you feel fear rising, another thing you can do is to look in the mirror and tell yourself that you're not afraid. You can do this!

Fear is the enemy of hope. We all have hopes and dreams. Being afraid to take a chance and go after those goals is something you can conquer! Your situation is not hopeless. Be hopeful and believe in yourself. What's stopping you? Do you fear that if you ask for what you want, the answer will be no? You have to have faith in yourself, your abilities, and your thoughts. Having faith is such a huge factor in overcoming fear. If you don't have faith in yourself, you can't possibly believe that you can be successful at anything, especially something you're afraid of. The Bible has so many verses about fear. We're going to cover that in a later chapter. But for now, I want you to think about your faith. Do you have faith in yourself?

Chapter 1 Challenge

At the end of each chapter, I'm going to challenge you. And for this chapter, I want you to think about your fears. Ask yourself these questions:

1. What fears do I have?

2. Which of these fears are natural? (i.e., spiders/heights/public speaking)

3. Which of these fears are deeper rooted?

4. What has happened to make these fears so powerful?

5. How are these fears affecting my life?

6. Do I need help?

Don't be afraid to delve deep into these questions. In order to live fearlessly, you have to understand what's causing your fears. The first step is acknowledging your fears and discovering the root cause.

Sometimes root causes are very easy to figure out. If they're not, don't be discouraged and don't be afraid to get help. A Life Coach is the perfect person to help you discover your roadblocks so you can experience your breakthrough. That's what we do.

Testimony

I Was Different

I had always been told as a child that I looked different, I wasn't pretty, I was too tall, and I wasn't smart. As a teenager, I started to believe those things too. I spoke those words to myself and carried them over to adulthood. When I had a family of my own, the hurt and pain I felt from rejection carried over to my children. I had let what people said about me control my future.

I always wanted to become a real estate agent because it was a glamorous and lucrative career, but I always managed to talk myself out of taking the class, thinking I wasn't smart enough to pass the test. I had a victim mentality. I had become wounded by what others had to say about me. It was so bad that I would criticize myself before others had an opportunity to do so to lessen the pain of rejection.

After years of struggling with depression and anxiety, I finally came to terms with the truth that I am who God wants me to be. I am made in His image. God makes no mistakes and therefore, I am not a mistake.

My attitude started to slowly change but it required prayer to learn to love myself. My relationship with my husband and children changed and I became more loving and giving. I was no longer the victim. I was able to let my inner beauty flourish and I believed that I could do all things through God who strengthens me.

After several years, I became a senior manager at the local hospital. I also opened a restaurant. Finally I took the Real Estate Exam and passed it on the first time. Now, I am the real estate agent that I always wanted to be! Through prayer, I was able to release the enemy's strongholds over my life. I'll never talk about what I can't do anymore because with God all things are possible.

~ F. K. W.

The only thing we have to fear is fear itself.

~ Franklin Roosevelt

CHAPTER 2

FACE IT HEAD ON

Now that we've figured out what's causing the fear, we need to work on facing the fear. This is not always an easy feat. Facing fear is the same as confronting an enemy, but it's also very necessary for growth. Depending on the fear, it can take some time. These are not quick fixes, and they're not meant to be.

Recent polls tell us that 95 percent of all people struggle with fear and self-confidence, and it's something you will deal with for the rest of your life. Don't be discouraged though; just recognize that it may take some time to tackle each one. If it's something simple like scary movies, overcoming that is easy—don't watch scary movies!

What about a deep-rooted fear? How can you deal with that? Well, you can start by facing it head on. Don't run from the fear. When you start feeling the fear come over you, stop what you're doing and pay attention to the feeling. Think about the fear and what it's doing to you in that moment. Take a deep breath. Now ask yourself, "Why am I so afraid?" Don't wait until it is so overwhelming that it feels insurmountable. Stop and confront it as soon as you feel the fear building up. The quicker you recognize it, the quicker you can deal with it.

I use prayer. My faith helps me deal with a lot of fears. The Bible talks about fear and how to overcome it. I also turn to scripture a lot. One of my favorites is: "Be not afraid of them [their faces], for I am with you to deliver you, says the Lord" (Jeremiah 1:8 Amplified).

Another technique that works for me is asking myself how it will affect me now and in the long term. If it's something that's not going to matter a week from now, I'm not going to let it control me.

If you have a fear of switching careers, it's very normal to be afraid of the uncertainties associated with such an event. That's a life changer, but you still need to deal with it. You can work through this by reviewing the pros and cons of your current career, as opposed to the career you want to go into. If the pros outweigh the cons after doing that, then push the fears to the back of your mind and go for it.

A former co-worker had been contemplating for months whether she should leave the company and pursue another place of employment or stay and make it work. She finally made the decision to go for it, and she has not regretted it for a moment. Once she worked through the fear, she went for it!

Please keep in mind that change is not easy. Sometimes we fight things we know we need because of fear. Most people do not like change. In fact, most people detest it. Overcoming fear may force you to change some things in your life. Don't let that discourage you; just don't give up. And if there is more than one fear, deal with the most pressing one first.

One coaching client wanted to do a complete overhaul in his life. He wanted to switch careers, improve relationships, and engage in personal development—all at the same time. I explained to him that taking on all of this at once could be counter-productive and overwhelming, so we decided to take one step at a time. The most important change for him was a career change, so we dealt with that first.

He had several fears. He felt like he was too old, and he didn't think he wanted to stay in the same field. He wasn't sure what he wanted to do—should he start his own company or work for someone else? So we wrote down each fear and dealt with them one at a time.

1. He was afraid that he was too old to leave his current career and start over.
2. He was scared to try something new.
3. He was dealing with the fear of starting his own company.
4. He was afraid he wouldn't find anything else if he left his current company.

We covered each fear and he dealt with each one of them. His fear of age was about finding an excuse to stay where he was. I explained that you're never too old to start over. Colonel Sanders was sixty-five years old when he started Kentucky Fried Chicken! So don't be afraid of your age. Like I told my client, age is just a number.

Then we tackled his fear of switching careers. After some coaching, he realized that he liked what he was doing, but he didn't enjoy working for his current company. So we killed two birds with one stone. He didn't want to start his own company; he just wanted a change. So that's what he did. He got another job. When we broke everything down and he was encouraged—by me, his Life Coach—to face his fears head on, he realized that they weren't as bad as he thought. Once he was able to name them and work through them, he overcame them and moved forward. This did not happen quickly. We worked together for over a year to accomplish these goals. He is still working through some things, but the most important thing is that his fear of facing the hurdles is gone. He can confidently move forward knowing that it is possible to overcome his life challenges. You might find yourself in a similar situation. If so, use the techniques that my client used to help you face the fear head on.

MYTH – Extraordinary people allow their fears to determine what actions they take in life.

FACT – Extraordinary people do not let their fears control their lives. They push past it and move forward.

When I decided to be a Life Coach, I knew I wanted to help people. There was one big obstacle—I had worked in finance for over fifteen years and I was very comfortable in it. But I also knew it wasn't my purpose. So I prayed a lot, took the courses, and became certified. It was scary trying to build a Life Coaching practice, writing a blog, raising three teenagers, and trying to rebuild my life after a divorce. But facing it head on and not letting fear win enabled me to move forward in my career, even though I was completely terrified and was moving into uncharted territory. I discovered great courage in taking action. You can, too.

Don't let fear hold you back from achieving your dreams and goals. Face it head on. We're all afraid of making the "wrong" decision. But learn to see it differently. Look at your options carefully, but don't overanalyze them.

If something doesn't go the way you planned, don't focus on the bad in the situation. Figure out what you learned and what you can take away from it. Your perspective on the situation will determine where you go. If you only see the bad, you're not going to learn anything. If you change your perspective and look at what you learned from it, it becomes growth.

One of my favorite quotes is from Thomas Edison: "I have not failed. I've found 10,000 ways that won't work." Imagine where we'd be today if he gave up before he got to that ten thousandth time. And if you don't think you have the "right" education, he was a high school dropout! Don't ever say it's impossible or you can't get past the fear. Trust me; you can.

MYTH – Most people are unafraid of taking risks, which could dramatically improve the quality of their lives.

FACT – Even successful people are afraid of taking risks. But they don't allow that to stop them.

Chapter 2 Challenge

1. What am I facing today?

2. Can I face that fear head on so I can move past the fear?

3. What will I gain when I get through the fear?

4. How bad do I want it?

Testimony

My Fear of Success

What do we have to be afraid of? Isaiah 41:10 tells us, "Do not fear, for I am with you." God's Word is what I choose to live by, but the truth is I have not always gone to God first for my direction. In fact, I can honestly say more times than not that I have attempted to figure things out on my own, and that is one way fear can easily creep into your life.

Fear is the one thing that can defeat us. We are not necessarily defeated by what others say to us, or what others think of us. That defeat comes when we allow our own fears to take over our thoughts in what we decide to be afraid of.

Several years ago I experienced a huge sense of fear—I was afraid of success and it caused me extreme anxiety. I know we hear about people who are afraid to fail, so they overcompensate, or take on more than they can handle, but in this case, I could clearly see the finish line and all that came with it, and it caused me to almost experience a nervous breakdown!

For many years, I had my own business as a makeup consultant and loved every minute of it! I was so passionate about teaching women about skin care and helping them to learn the proper way to apply and use the many different products that suited them. In short, I loved making women feel better about how they looked. Because I truly loved what I was doing, others wanted to do it too, so I shared the opportunity with many other women and with a lot of hard work, soon was on my way to building a unit and becoming a director with an awesome company. As with any road to the top, you work hard, and then you work harder to achieve the goals you set for yourself. Naturally, I knew what was expected and I worked very hard. I was well within my frame—heading toward the finish line. I continued to run my business and share the opportunity with others, but the closer I got to the end of that road, the more I began to feel a level of extreme anxiety I find difficult to explain. This awful feeling began to take over my thoughts, and I began to suffer both emotionally and physically. What was once a very deliberate movement toward my planned goal soon became very non-intentional actions to destroy all that I had built. Talk about a 360!

At some point in this awful decline, I realized some things about myself. I realized I may not be able to handle all the new, and much bigger responsibilities that I would have; I realized people would expect more from me; and I realized that maybe I was not ready to be a big-time director. You see, I began to think I had not worked hard enough to have what the other directors had…so this was not for me. I realized I was afraid to "make it"; I realized I was just not ready. The *reality* of what I was doing began to look like something I could not handle, so I stopped doing what worked and began making stupid decisions—decisions good leaders don't make. I allowed my fears to take over and consume me and I quit.

Fear can be totally overwhelming if you allow it to be. I said at the beginning that I choose to live by God's Word. I know that I can "do all things through Christ who gives me strength" (Phil. 4:13) and that "when I am weak, He is strong" (1 Tim 1:16.). I also know that nothing is too much for the God I serve, so I should never feel overwhelmed by fear because the God I serve said He would never leave me.

So, what have I learned through all of this? I learned to always breathe first, and then pray. I have learned to never give up on anything but to go to God for everything! I learned to take a moment to recall what I have already accomplished and to reflect on how that was done. I can do nothing without my Heavenly Father, and I have learned that I can help others deal with their fear of success by sharing what I know.

First, acknowledge your fear. It is real! I didn't know what I know now, so I gave in to the physical illnesses and the emotional exhaustion I experienced. Next, take inventory of what is going on, so you can understand where it is coming from. Had I done that, I would have realized I was slowly sabotaging my business and maybe I could have prevented that from happening.

Lastly, work to find ways to overcome your fears. It can be done. I was just scared to be the successful director I was working hard to become. I honestly believed it was not God's will for me to "make it." What I learned from experiencing this type of "fear" was that I should trust God in *all* situations. I could not allow the world to convince me I was not capable of doing what God has destined for me. Determined to succeed, I returned to school and completed not one, but two degrees in a matter of eighteen months! If you feel like fear is taking over something you are trying to accomplish, do not procrastinate on actions you must take! Just do it—you will feel so much better once you take the steps to get it done, and then you will realize success in completing your goals!

~ A. Utley

Fear stifles our thinking and actions. It creates indecisiveness that results in stagnation.

~ Charles Stanley

CHAPTER 3

HAVE A PLAN

Having a plan is something that should part of your daily life, for every area of your life. Goal-setting can help you overcome fear. By writing your plan and following it, each time you check something off your list—big or small—you build more confidence to tackle the next goal or challenge.

I have a one-year, five-year, and even a ten-year plan. There are some really big goals on there! But I believe and have faith that I can achieve all of them, even the ones that are huge and daunting.

My pastor recently asked our congregation if we had a five-year plan, and I was surprised that not even 10 percent raised their hand. That's a lot of people with no goals or plans. And that's pretty scary.

I encourage all of my clients to complete a plan; there are several great reasons to have a plan and follow it. By keeping your eyes on the prize and not on the obstacles, you don't focus on the fear. When you write out your goals and can see the vision, it should get you so excited that you're willing to do whatever it takes—including pushing through the fear to reach it! It's also not just about you. It's about the people who will benefit from your gift. Imagine the lives you can influence by sharing your God-given talent, your time, and your treasure. When you accomplish your goals, you are helping others as well—your family, friends, your community, and, of course, your company, if it's career related.

Success takes work. It's not going to happen overnight. Having a plan and checking off your to-do list will make you feel accomplished. For me, the more I check off, the more excited I get about checking off the next thing.

MYTH – Writing down your fears just makes them more visible.

FACT – Making a list of your fears is a great way to "see" them, and to work through them.

You have to keep moving when you produce this plan. You can write the plan in the beginning, but it won't do any good if you don't take action. Following through is key. Your mindset will play a role in this as well. Your plan will have to change and adjust based on the completion of goals.

How to Set Goals

1) Think about the overall picture of what you want to accomplish. Write it down. I can't stress how important this is. Writing the goals down help them become real.

2) Break down your goals into smaller more

manageable goals if you need to. Doing this will help diminish the fear of such a big goal being unconquerable. Breaking it down will make it less overwhelming.

3) Put a due date on your goals. Giving yourself a time limit does two things: It helps you to set and reach goals, and it keeps you on track.

4) Get in the habit of writing down daily goals. It may take a while to get into the habit and may seem daunting at first, but having your daily goals written down will help you get to your big goals. Keep in mind that daily goals are not the same as your big goals. Daily goals should be completed daily so you accomplish your overall goals.

5) Don't be afraid to ask for help. You're not alone in this. Don't feel like you have to take this on by yourself. If you know someone who is constantly reaching their goals, talk to them and find out what works for them.

As doors open, and as your direction becomes clear, you have to be willing to be flexible. This can cause fear. Most people don't like change. They don't adjust well. They like routine and for things to be the same. But what they should really be afraid of is the mediocrity that they'll settle for because of fear.

Don't be afraid to be better. Keep moving, keep pushing, and keep believing. As you move from goal to goal, your fear will decrease. Every hurdle will become easier to deal with. If you have big goals, you might have big fears. Don't let that stop you! Focus on the goal; not on what's happening today. You're a conqueror and an over-comer. Always remember that. As you check the goals off and overcome each fear, celebrate! You've accomplished something big! Overcoming any fear is worth celebrating. If you remember to celebrate the small victories, it gives you courage to face the next challenge.

MYTH – People think that planning and fantasizing is action.

FACT – When we're trying to move past fear; we spend way too much time analyzing it before taking any action. Just do it!

If you have a desire to start your own business, but you've been afraid, do it anyway. You need to make a plan, take your time, and do it step by step. If you fail, then at least you can say you tried, and now you know what doesn't work. Just regroup and keep going. Many entrepreneurs will tell you that they were not successful in the first business adventure. But the key is they didn't give up. They kept going until they were successful. Just taking the first step is huge in overcoming fear.

Whatever steps you take to overcome your fear, be happy and be proud of yourself. In fact, by reading this book, you've admitted you're afraid of something and you're taking a step to be better!

The feeling you get when you overcome a fear is something you'll want to feel over and over again. It's a great feeling! Having a plan, writing it down, taking action, pushing past the fear, and meeting goal after goal are reasons to celebrate!

Chapter 3 Challenge

1. Do you have a one-year, five-year and ten-year plan?

2. What obstacles, if any, can stop you?

3. Do you have a plan to overcome those obstacles?

4. Can you be flexible in your plans and goals and adapt to change when necessary?

Testimony

This Was Not My Original Plan

Being seventeen is scary enough. Being seventeen and pregnant is the toughest fear I've faced so far. It was completely unplanned. I took the first two tests at my boyfriend's house so I could avoid having to tell him later. The first one was positive, so I drank another bottle of water and took a second one just to confirm. Sure enough, the second one was positive as well. I told my boyfriend it was yes, and we just looked at each other. We were both in shock, and finally he said, "It is what it is." I, on the other hand, was still in shock, and my mind and heart were racing. How was I going to tell my mom? How was I going to tell my dad? Thoughts like these continued to roll around my head.

I was in total denial, and I ended up buying two more tests. Both positive. Two more weeks went by and I told myself it was time to tell my mom, so I took two more tests the morning I decided to tell her. They were both positive, of course. There was no doubt about me being pregnant now, and there was nothing else to do, but tell her. I don't believe in abortion and adoption was questionable. I asked my boyfriend how he felt about both, and he said neither was an option as far as he was concerned.

So, here I am seventeen years old, confirming my life for the next eighteen-plus years. I stood in my room with the positive pregnancy tests in one hand, and my college acceptance letter in the other.

As far as high school went, I didn't start showing until five-and-a-half months. I did tell a few people so there wouldn't be rumors. Luckily it was my senior year and the baby wasn't due until after graduation. Since I had already gotten accepted into college, I had to decide the next course to take. I decided to not give up on college, but to postpone it by one semester because I want to get used to being a mom.

My beautiful son is now a week and a half old. Even though the last year has brought some of the scariest moments in my life, I love my son with all my heart, and I couldn't be happier with him.

~ A. Sanchez

We are afraid of the enormity of the possible.

~ Emile M. Cloran

CHAPTER 4

TALK ABOUT IT

When dealing with fear, it's very easy to keep everything inside. In today's society, it's not cool to admit that we're not perfect or that we need help. But that's not the best attitude to take. When you open up and share the fear with someone you trust, you realize that you're not alone! Knowing that you're not alone and you're not the only one experiencing fear is such a relief.

Fear is a mindset and it can be overcome. We all face fear, and that's why we should turn to people around us that we can trust and can share things with. They help us deal with our daily lives, and even though we don't like to discuss fear, we need to get it out. The more we hold it inside, the more it continues to build. Once you're "full," you will explode and it will manifest in ways that are undesirable. If you hate your job and every day is miserable, you'll come home from work and take it out on your family. You may be unhappy in your personal life and as a result, you take it out on your co-workers or your friends. Again, you may not even realize what you're doing. You just know that you're unhappy. What you want to do is deal with it in a way that's productive and helpful, not harmful.

There are times when I can talk myself through the fear I'm facing. It all depends on the fear and how intense it is. Sometimes it helps to write about it. I keep a journal and I write down just about everything that's important to me—that includes my fears. When I go back and read it later, sometimes I laugh at myself. Often I'll find that something I once was completely terrified of doesn't seem so overwhelming after I've thought it through.

When I first started working out, I was afraid to go the gym. I wasn't in "shape" and I didn't want to be judged by all the perfect super-models. So I did everything possible to not go. When my friend said she wanted a workout buddy, I said I would give it a try. I was still so afraid of stepping in that gym but I talked to her about it and she helped me realized that it wouldn't be as bad as I thought. When I got there, I realized that very few people there were in perfect shape, and it was not so intimidating after all.

MYTH – To be effective in dealing with fear, one has to hide, deny, or get rid of their fear.

FACT – The best way to deal with fear is to talk about it and face it, not to deny it exists.

Before I became a public speaker, just thinking about being on stage terrified me! The thought of standing in front of strangers and being so exposed was suffocating. I talked myself out of it for years. I just knew that everyone would judge me, that I wasn't good enough. So I came up with many reasons why I couldn't do it. But the reality was (which I wouldn't admit at the time) that I was afraid. I finally wised up and talked to a friend about it who also happens to be a speaker. He told me he experiences the exact same thing. That's right, present tense! He's been speaking for years, and he still gets a little nervous before he preaches.

I thought since he's been preaching for years, he wouldn't have a fear of speaking. It felt good to know that what I was feeling was normal. With his help, I was able to get up the courage to face my fear. We still encourage each other and that is a great benefit of sharing fears with other people.

I have another friend who went through something devastating and terrifying—her husband committed suicide. She had no idea anything was wrong and he showed no signs of depression. Still, his choice made her a single mother to their son. Having people she could turn to and talk about this is what got her through. She is blessed with great family members and friends and the fear and hurt she felt was easier to deal with. While it is very hard to understand why someone commits suicide, if she didn't have the support system she has, it would have made the situation much more difficult.

I can't imagine what she was going through. She was, however, strong enough to recognize that she couldn't get through it alone and her faith in God helped her recover from this devastating period in her life.

MYTH – Most people are fearless about being authentic and real.

FACT – Being your authentic, true self should never make you afraid! You are unique and different for a reason.

Chapter 4 Challenge

My challenge to you for this chapter is simple to say, but requires a little trust to put it into action: Don't keep your fear inside. If you're afraid to talk about it, write it down. I really encourage you to talk about your fears with someone you trust.

1) Do I have people in my life that I trust and can talk to?

2) Is sharing my fears with someone the worst thing that can happen?

3) Am I too embarrassed to share my fears with a Life Coach, counselor, or pastor?

Testimony

Speaking, or the Fear Thereof

Before my twenty-first birthday, I was in a relationship where I fathered and lost a child under what became criminal circumstances. I was investigated and exonerated of any wrongdoing in the death of my, to date, only child. Yet, I lived in fear of being recognized, being thought of differently, and of a past that is now more than half a lifetime gone.

The fear has lessened over the years. I have grown comfortable with who I am. I've learned to accept the things that happened to me and realized that the circumstances didn't make me who I am. What makes me who I am are the lessons about perseverance in the face of adversity. I began to realize that there was no perceived "Scarlet Letter" emblazoned on me for the world to see. Yes, there are times, especially when meeting new people, that I get a bit nervous about what their reaction might be if they learn of my past. Then I realize that the reaction is theirs. If they ask about my life, I tell them the truth, warts and all. It truly does set you free.

When it comes to fearing for our survival, most people have some type of fear that they aren't going to be able to provide for the ones they love. Part of my fear stems from being told that hardship may always be lurking around every corner. I grew up very close to my Depression Era grandparents. I watched them borderline horde things to make sure they "had enough." It was a big influence on a small child. As I grew, I would always carry what I thought I needed with me. I had a backpack that would make an Army Ranger look unprepared. I carried it everywhere and it was completely stocked for any and all emergencies. I thought it was my way of dealing with fear. Actually, that backpack was symbolic of many things.

From one perspective, it was my proof that I could overcome all challenges. Also, it was a bit of a security blanket. It helped me to feel that I could face the world. There was another part of it that I thought was independence. I didn't have to rely on anyone but myself and my backpack. I even got others to rely on my having my backpack fully stocked for any challenge.

I finally realized it was just weight—the physical embodiment of the emotional weight and fear of failure. I'd like to say that there was some eureka moment of mental alacrity which brought me to this conclusion, but I'd be lying. It was really a very smart friend who asked me, "Why do you always carry that thing around?" When I gave her the reasons, she simply said, "What can go wrong that we can't solve together?" She basically told me that no matter what, there is always someone who is there and you aren't alone. She forced me to look at my fear and realize how much it weighed me down, both physically and emotionally. So, one day I went to the grocery store without it.

The more I left it at home, the more I realized that I didn't need to have it with me at all times. Just because it wasn't there didn't mean that something bad was going to happen. It was a lesson I needed to learn through repetition and by creating new habits. That mental and physical retraining provided me with the tools I needed to remove a lot of weight and fear, physically and emotionally.

The last fear is, in my opinion, the worst that you can ever face. It's also the one I tend to struggle with the most. It's the fear of failure that comes from not believing in yourself. That type of fear can lead to a paralysis of the mind and body, which leaves you at the mercy of everything life can throw at you. I think it's a common theme in one way or another for everyone. Situation X appears and we begin to doubt ourselves and our abilities. Then that carries over to Situation Y and we begin to lose faith in everything we have learned and the lessons we have taught ourselves about overcoming adversity.

Every new challenge that life presents gives you a moment to do something special— a chance to prove that you were up to the challenge and you didn't take it lying down. As William Jennings Bryant, former Secretary of the United States said, "Destiny is no matter of chance, it's a matter of choice."

When you choose to submit to your fear, you take away your choice. Today, control the challenge; don't let it control you.

~ A. Merzke

Ultimately we know deeply that the
other side of every fear is freedom.

~ Marilyn Ferguson

CHAPTER 5

POSITIVE AFFIRMATIONS

How do you feel when your favorite song comes on the radio? What about when you hear something inspiring? It's really hard to be fearful and down when you hear something that pumps you up.

Athletes have rituals to get them pumped for the game. As an athlete, I listen to great music that gets me pumped up and excited for my games or my workout. I also use positive affirmations.

One of my favorite authors and speakers is Jim Rohn; he encourages speaking positive affirmations to overcome fears. Positive affirmations are just saying positive things over and over, either right in a row or daily. I use both and it depends on what's going on. If I'm facing something critical and I need uplifting right then and there, I repeat the affirmation over and over. Otherwise, I have a daily routine of speaking uplifting messages to myself.

When I'm getting ready in the morning, I look in the mirror and I say, "I'm beautiful. I'm smart. I'm healthy. I'm loved. I'm very blessed. I can do whatever it is I put my mind to, and nothing and no one can hold me back!" I say that in the mirror every single day and it really does work!

So how can speaking positive affirmations help you cope with fear? If this practice didn't work, books like *The Secret* by Rhonda Byrne or *Awaken the Giant* by Tony Robbins would not be bestsellers. Both of these books (and many more) encourage positive affirmations that include thinking and speaking positive things over your life. They help you overcome fear, but that's not all. Positive Affirmations also help you deal with other issues in your life like low self-esteem, finances, weight, business, and relationships.

Use some of the ones I use or write down your own and make them specific to your life. Tell yourself that the fear is not real, that you can overcome it, and that you can solve the problem.

When you get in the habit of speaking positive things over your life, it will soon become second nature and the fear won't seem so big. We are often so used to letting the fear take control and send us over the edge, when it should be the other way around. You should take control of the fear!

MYTH – Only a few people are driven by the fear of what others might discover about them.

FACT – You should never be afraid of what people might discover about you. Be transparent.

I've struggled with my weight for a very long time. I had this awful fear that I was going to have a heart attack in my forties like my mom. I would let myself get so worked up and afraid that I truly let the fear cripple me. Finally, I realized that I have some control over this situation! I might not be able to control the genetic part of it, but I can control my eating, activity level, and do whatever else I can to prevent a heart attack.

The most amazing thing is that when I go to the doctor, he always tells me that my heart is in great shape. It was just my own fear! Now when those thoughts come, I say I'm healthy, I eat better, and I exercise. I'm not going to have a heart attack. This is not some huge epiphany, but it works! I feel better and, most importantly, I feel in control and not afraid. Every time I work out, I feel awesome! Even if I don't lose another pound, I know that I'm still practicing healthy habits. I have the fear under control.

A very dear friend struggled with low self-esteem. At one point, she was very heavy, and didn't feel like she could ever lose weight. She was afraid to even try. She struggled with this issue for years!

One day she was reading about positive affirmations. She hung her affirmations on her bathroom mirror and when she got ready for work, she recited them every day. She told herself that she was beautiful just the way she was, but that she was going to eat healthier. She wanted to be alive to play with her kids. She took it slow and stopped putting pressure on herself to lose weight. Instead, she decided to make small changes. She lost twenty-six pounds! All of that happened because she decided to speak positive affirmations that helped her overcome her fear of trying to be healthy.

You can do this, too, in whatever area of your life you're struggling with—your career, your weight, or your relationships. When you're able to think positive, you're not crippled by fear. Instead, you start to focus on the possibilities.

MYTH – There is very little anyone can do to remove the unwarranted grip that fear places on personal effectiveness.

FACT – When you give fear a place in your mind, it destroys your willingness to be the most effective person you can be.

My challenge to you for this chapter is this: Whenever you feel fearful about something, just start reciting positive affirmations. Not just once, but all day—even when you're not fearful of anything at all. Pretty soon it will be a habit, and you'll be more in control and less fearful.

Chapter 5 Challenge

1. What's the *real* reason for my anxiety?
2. What can I do right now to get started, in spite of the fear?
3. What affirmations can I recite daily, weekly, or monthly to become fearless?

Testimony

Overcoming the Fear of Man and Finding My Voice

My biggest challenge was to overcome the fear of man. I was afraid to tell people what I really felt and allowed them to control my thoughts and actions. I went along with things that I did not want to do or agree with things I didn't agree with, all because I failed to have courage to speak up and speak out. It left me unhappy and torn most of the time. I wanted to fit in and I wanted everyone to like me. On rare occasions when I would voice how I felt or rejected something that was not right, I would be criticized by family and friends or I would be rejected all together. This kept me from speaking out and being myself.

As time went on I built up a lot of resentment and developed the attitude no one will tell me what to do anymore. I cut off everyone. I stopped talking to certain friends and even family members. This did not make me feel any better—it made me feel worse because I was not this person either and my conscience was eating me up. I had become a people pleaser, but I was slowly losing my identity at the same time.

One day a wonderful friend paid me a visit. She was older and wise. As we talked, she said, "You have a friend who will never mistreat you, who will allow you to be yourself, despite your shortcomings. And you will become a better person each time you are with this person." I wondered who the heck this person was because I wanted to meet them now. Then she said, "It is your Creator. That is the only friend who matters and who you should please. Not man!"

That talk changed my life. Once I strengthened my relationship with my God and, my life turned upside down for the better. I was able to express myself and over time I learned to say no and be okay with that. The more I was honest with myself and others, I felt better. I did not worry about what others said as much and when I did I prayed about it.

There were others who were not used to this side of me, and they had to learn the new me. I also ended friendships that were not beneficial to either of us. This change was a gradual process and it was tough trying to change deeply entrenched habits, but I learned that the antidote of fear of man is strong faith in God.

Jehovah God gave me the courage I thought I never possessed. I asked Him for help and He gave me what I needed, but it was up to me to follow through and He had the patience to wait until I got it. This new process brought true friends and better relationships. I have a good conscience and I have peace. Though this was a hard walk, I was able to let go of a lot of weight on my shoulders and keep true to myself and embrace rejection, even if it cost me my pride for the moment. It helped me give back what God gave me: love and honesty.

~ F. Futrell

Courage is resistance to fear,
mastery of fear, not absence of fear.

~ Mark Twain

CHAPTER 6

Faith and Fear

This chapter is extremely important, especially when dealing with fear. Having super crazy faith when dealing with fear is the absolute best thing you can have. You have to believe in yourself and have faith in yourself. Fear is just Satan trying to get you off your game and keep you from reaching your destiny. How does that work? It happens when you're so afraid of something (losing your job, having kids, being alone, writing a book, public speaking) that either you just give up on your destiny, or you settle for the next best thing because you're afraid to go for the best.

You don't want regrets. You don't want the "shoulda, coulda, wouldas." Why settle for second best when you can have the best?

Here's a confession for you: I didn't always have faith in myself. And I can't honestly tell you that my faith is at an all-time high every single day, even now, because it isn't. I need God, I need prayer, and I need faith to get me through every single day. I also understand that believing in myself and choosing not to settle for second are all aspects of having faith. I still have doubts sometimes. This is normal, but I don't ever let it render me incapable of growth or movement!

I have a friend who recently dealt with fear concerning his career. He's been at the same company for twelve years and has been going through a tough time at work. So he decided to start looking elsewhere. When he got a job offer, he was hesitant at first to take it. He'd been at his current company for so long, and while no job is completely guaranteed, he felt some sense of security at his old company.

MYTH – Conquering a big fear is the most important decision.

FACT – Facing any size fear is a big deal.

Changing companies is not an easy decision. The fear of change, moving to a different company, the sense of comfort, and giving up your benefits (or at least changing them) is enough to make anyone stressed.

When he discussed it with his wife, at first she was hesitant, too. But he prayed about it. He didn't rush to make a decision. He thought about it for a few days, spoke to his wife about it, and together they made a decision that was best for them. He decided to take the job. The fact that he relied on his faith and decided to move past the fear into the unknown, is such a great example of how you can push through your circumstances and take a chance!

The phrase "do not be afraid" is written in the Bible 365 times. There are so many verses about being fearless. One of the clear points the Bible touches on more than once is how we too often are afraid of man, as opposed to trusting God. One of my favorite verses is Proverbs 29:25 (NKJV): "The fear of man brings a snare, but whoever trusts in the LORD shall be safe."

MYTH – Holding onto something we have no control over is empowering.

FACT – Not letting go weakens us; it does not help us overcome fear.

Even when you have small tinges of doubt, it's still doubt. God asks us to have faith as small as a mustard seed. That's just a little bit of faith. But that shows Him that you trust and believe in Him. Remind yourself daily that God wants you to succeed. You were not given a spirit of fear, but of a sound mind. Use that and the many other scriptures about fear to help you when fear comes knocking. Remember, fear is (F)alse (E)vidence (A)ppearing (R)eal. You are an overcomer!

These days, when the fear comes and I feel helpless and afraid, I just start reciting the Word of God and remind myself that God is in control. I pray about it and let it go. I'm not saying it's easy and that everything will be perfect immediately, but take it one day at a time. Even when you get over your current fear, it's not gone forever. There will always be something. So don't think that you'll just pray once and it's done. Keep reciting positive affirmations and going to the Word. This is a lifetime commitment.

Chapter 6 Challenge

1. How strong is my faith?

2. When I think about the fears I'm experiencing, do I feel like they are God-given fears or man-made fears?

3. Am I satisfied with being mediocre?

4. Do I trust God?

Testimony

Faith Through Fear

Our world was shaken. We took our six-year-old daughter, Alexis, to the doctor for a swollen elbow. In a twenty-four-hour period, we went from the pediatrician, to the pediatric orthopedics' office, to the children's emergency room, and were finally admitted to Vanderbilt Children's Hospital. My wife and I thought that our daughter had an infection or fracture in the elbow that was causing her a lot of pain. We were devastated to find out, after multiple tests, that our daughter was diagnosed with Leukemia—B-ALL. Neither my wife nor I knew much about this disease. All we knew is that our daughter had cancer. My wife was in tears. I was mostly in a state of shock and bewilderment.

After receiving this information from the doctor, we had to tell our daughter. But how? My wife and I put on our strongest poker faces, but instantly Alexis knew something wasn't right with the remnants of tears still in our eyes. We knew, as any parent would, that we had to remain strong. But that strength did not come from us. Once we explained to our daughter that her blood was sick, we immediately lifted her up to God in prayer. We placed her healing and our faith in Him. Clearly, we know we have no control or power over this thing called cancer. So, we had to hand it over to the One who does.

In the next week, we all gained a broader knowledge of what Leukemia is, the medicines used to fight it, and what to expect for the next two and a half years. We were in it for the long haul. We shed a lot of tears explaining this diagnosis to our friends and family. But, little did we know, we would cry even more tears of joy because of the love shown to us by our family, friends, and co-workers.

During this time, it was hard to even plan the next meal or how to get our oldest daughter to school and back. But God provided us an immense network of people who picked up the loose ends in every area. People gave us comfort, brought us food, gave us money, and gift cards. Both of my daughters had the absolute biggest Christmas ever thanks to their school, churches, family, and friends. What really touched us was that a lot of these gifts came from people who didn't know us or my daughter. But I guess Christians don't have to know each other to still show the love of Christ.

Alexis is a very brave little girl. Her faith rests in God for her healing. She has gone to multiple clinic visits and hospital stays, and is always looking to find a friend to play with in the hall. The idea of her being sick doesn't keep her down.

On day twenty-nine, Alexis was in remission after a bone marrow biopsy. We were ecstatic and praised God for her continued healing. About a week later, we got a call from the doctor. He explained that while Alexis was in remission, further testing showed that she had a genetic marker (Hypodiploid). Typically, patients with Hypodiploid are not in remission on day twenty-nine and the next course of action is an immediate bone marrow transplant. One of the doctors had gone to a conference one month prior and learned about treating patients with this genetic marker with chemo, rather than a bone marrow transplant.

The doctors utilized their network of Leukemia specialists across the U.S. and around the globe. All of them had opinions, but there was no conclusive data to support whether Alexis should continue chemotherapy or undergo a bone marrow transplant. The decision to continue chemo or transplant was placed in mine and my wife's hands. Quite frankly, this sucked. For us, it was so easy to simply rely on God for Alexis's healing, but now we had to make a huge decision.

Again, we lifted this up to God, but this time we had to wait for His response. We had a few weeks to decide, thankfully. Even without making a rushed decision, it weighed heavily. My wife and I preferred chemo, as the bone marrow transplant had so many risks and would include a two- to three-month hospital stay. But, ultimately we needed God's Word.

In praise and worship at church one Wednesday night, God spoke to me. After I sang, "Take me deeper than my feet could ever wander," God told me that it does not matter which treatment Alexis does. He said, "I have healed her." I was moved to my knees with his Word. Here we were looking for an A or B answer. God showed me that night that He doesn't work within the confines of this earthly realm.

All of the stress of this decision melted away completely. So much so that I even told the doctor that I'd even be okay with option C (walking away with no treatment). Of course, Alexis's doctor doesn't work within the spiritual realm, so that option was quickly shut down. My wife and I decided to continue with chemotherapy instead of transplanting. However, the doctors wanted to do another bone marrow biopsy five months in from diagnosis, to make sure they had advised us correctly. We told them they would not find anything, because our God had healed Alexis.

One week later we were able to again give God all the glory. They did not find any leukemia or Hypodiploid cells.

We know our God has healed our little girl. We don't say that our daughter has Leukemia. We can only say that she was simply diagnosed with it six months ago. All praise and glory to our Father in heaven and to His Son, who, by His stripes we are healed!

~ N. Bentley

Learn from the past, set vivid,
detailed goals for the future, and live
in the only moment of time over
which you have any control: now.

~ Denis Waitley

CHAPTER 7

This Is Just the Beginning

Now that you're prepared to deal with the fear, don't let yourself get into a "comfort" zone. Fear will always be there, but you will hopefully realize that you're not alone. We all struggle with fear, doubt, and anxiety. If you get nothing else from this book, I want you to know that you don't have to remain crippled by fear. You *can* work through it and overcome.

Everyone, and I mean everyone, is afraid of something. Just remember that you are now well equipped to deal with and conquer fear and to be everything you've wanted to be! You want to be successful in everything you do, and have a happy balanced life. Once you deal with your fears, you're well on your way to achieving those goals.

Here's a quick overview of what we've covered:

1. Fear is in your mind. You can overrule it!

2. Face fear head on. The quicker you deal with it, the easier it is to get over it.

3. Have a plan. When you're focused on your plan and not your problems, you'll be willing to do

whatever is necessary to make your goals and dreams a reality.

4. Talk about your fear with someone you trust. Sharing it and knowing you're not alone is a huge comfort and helps you deal with the situation.

5. Speak positive things over your life. You say it, repeat it, and believe it.

6. Trust Jesus! Have faith.

You're victorious! Keep thinking of yourself as fearless, unstoppable, and a giant! One of the best exercises is to imagine yourself exactly where you want to be. If that's as an entrepreneur, skinnier, smarter, promoted, or with a spouse and children, picture it!

Before I started speaking, I would picture myself in front of huge audiences speaking and empowering them. I would also picture myself at book signings and coaching individuals and groups. Being able to picture myself being exactly what I wanted to be and doing what I love, made me deal with fear, because I didn't want these goals to just be a dream. I wanted them to be reality.

How do you maintain the vision? Create a vision board!

I have a poster board with all of my goals, dreams, and ambitions on it. I have a picture of me speaking in front of a huge crowd. I have a picture of me in my office, and not at a corporate job. I have a bank statement with the amount I want to have in my savings account. I have a check that I want to write to one of the charities that I admire. Every day I see this collage of items and it keeps me motivated to keep moving forward.

What happens when I reach all of those goals? I set more goals! There will always be something on my board because I will never stop growing and evolving. And I will always have to conquer fears, especially as I step into unfamiliar territory and out of my comfort zone. But I refuse to let my fears keep me from reaching these goals.

When I'm coaching a new client it never ceases to surprise me that one of the top things on my client's list is the fear that they are facing. They're afraid of change, life, jobs, kids, relationships, health issues, and more. I've heard it all. When faced with fear, most of us want to run, hide, not think about it, and hope it goes away. That's not going to happen. It will still be there. You just have to be strong enough to know without a doubt that you can and will overcome the fear and be better.

Don't let past experiences keep you trapped. Push past the fear. Take action. Living in fear is not living at all. Move out of fear and be the great person you know that you are! Teach yourself to expect the best. Remember the positive affirmations? Make them a habit. You can learn to expect greatness.

Be open for new possibilities. When you open your heart and your mind and release the fear, the possibilities are endless! Remember to stay open to the possibilities. They can open a new pathway to your future.

Think of the worst thing that could possibly happen if you don't accomplish your goals. Now, visualize the best possible scenario if you accomplish all of your goals. Which one do you like better? Remember your power within.

Once you become fearless, you become limitless. Your dream is calling you. Are you going to answer?

Testimony

Facing Fear Head On

Overcoming fear is something we all have to deal with at some point in our lives. Let me tell you about one of my experiences with fear.

I was married for twenty-five years to an emotionally abusive husband who had many affairs during our marriage. Being a Christian, I always forgave him. We had three sons and later adopted a little girl. After a year and a half, I found out he had been molesting her. I left him and filed for divorce, but on the day I left, he threatened my life as I was leaving our house. Three weeks later, he kidnapped me and took me to a deserted hay barn to kill me.

At one point during my time as a hostage, I fell to my knees in the hay and cried out to God, "Father, I ask that somehow you get glory out of this." My husband pulled me up and I looked him in the eyes and from my heart I said, "I forgive you."

The Lord intervened. I was held hostage for six days until he was arrested and went to court for the sentencing on the child abuse charge. He was sentenced and immediately taken to jail.

I believe that I would not be alive if I had not forgiven him that night in the barn. When we don't forgive, we are not forgiven. Just like it says in Matthew 6:14–15, God cannot work in our behalf unless we forgive.

After being rescued, I moved in with my parents with my youngest son, but after my now ex-husband's court appearance, I began having nightmares and could not go to sleep at night. I would hear a noise and get up with a flashlight, looking in every space in my small bedroom, making sure my ex-husband was not there. Most of the spaces I looked in were so small that a human being could not possibly fit in it. I realized what I was doing was totally ridiculous, but fear had gripped me.

I prayed and asked God to help me overcome the fear. A few nights later as I was trying to go to sleep, I heart the Lord's voice in my spirit say, "I'll never let him do that to you again." At that moment I was totally set free from fear. I believe that walking in forgiveness opened the door for my healing and deliverance.

Psalms 34:4 (KJV)
"I sought the Lord, and he heard me, and delivered me from all my fears."

2 Timothy 1:7 (KJV)

"For God hath not given us the spirit of fear; but of power, and of love, and of a sound mind."

~ C. Mathis

ABOUT THE AUTHOR

Charletta Adams is an Author, Certified Professional Life Coach, and Speaker who is dedicated to helping people improve their lives, discover their value, and make aggressive and courageous life choices. She loves to help her clients discover their vision and purpose. Charletta has worked in finance for fifteen years and brings her business insight to her clients to help them successfully balance work and life.

Charletta lives in Nashville, Tennessee, and is the proud mom of three wonderful children. Connect with her at www.charlettaadams.com, and follow her blogs at www.charlettaadams.blogspot.com

93232530R10050

Made in the USA
Columbia, SC
11 April 2018